TURN OFF THE WIFI

& pick up

a Pen

A catalogue record for this book is available from the British Library.

Second Edition 2015.

First published in Great Britain in 2014 by Carpet Bombing Culture.

An imprint of Pro-actif Communications.

www.carpetbombingculture.co.uk

email: books@carpetbombingculture.co.uk

©Rhiannon Shove
www.burnafterwriting.me

ISBN: 978-1-908211-27-9

BURN AFTER WRITING
TEEN

THE PEN IS MIGHTIER THAN THE KEYBOARD

Handwriting, like a fingerprint or a singing voice - each one is unique. Each one betrays as much in itself as in the intention with which it is used. You give yourself away when you take pen to paper.

In an age of infinite and instant reproduction only the unique is still beautiful. Will your descendants ever read your Facebook Timeline?

Save something for the real world. Write something beautiful by hand and you are setting your thoughts free to last into eternity.

Welcome to an opportunity to face life's big questions.

Who are you now? How did you get here? Where are you going?

Burn After Writing offers probing questions, mind games,
thought experiments and homework assignments all on your
favourite subject - yourself.

Have fun with it, or take it too seriously, or both. It's up to you.

But when you finish with it make sure you bury it, hide it,
lock it up and run away . . . or Burn After Writing.

In a society where where we 'share' our everything, BAW goes against the grain
and politely asks you to 'share' nothing.

WELCOME TO THE BOOK OF YOU

Fate has brought you here. You have come to learn who you truly are through the secret mystic practice of answering loads of questions. Who says self-discovery cannot be a bit of a laugh?

Here is the only truly safe place you can talk about yourself non-stop without caring what anybody thinks (because there is nobody here but you). Everybody is always trying to tell you how to be - here you can tell the world what you really think with no consequences. Who is the real you? Maybe you will be surprised by what you find out . . .

This book will be a unique picture of you as you are right now, as you never will be again.

Here you will find questions designed to unlock the secrets of yourself. Answer them with courage and creativity. There are no wrong answers.

This is the practice session for the big interview exclusive you will doubtless face when the world finally discovers how amazing you actually are.

Use the power of the random factor to choose your questions. (That means flip through the book when you're bored.)

Or do the questions choose you?

Maybe one day, many years from now, you can use this trail of crumbs to find your way back home...

But wait!

Answer the questions! Interrogate yourself!
Get out of your comfort zone - and I don't mean sit on your sofa upside down. (Although by all means do so if you feel the need)

DISCLAIMER

If you are not you then you may not go further. For it is not written. You cannot simply skip in here without a care in the world and start prancing about the pages willy nilly. No. You must be initiated into the cult of B.A.W.

Before you go on, like the fool about to step off a cliff, stop here a moment and consider the sacred values of the cult of B.A.W.

- I WILL ANSWER WITH RELENTLESS, PAINFULLY SEARCHING HONESTY ALL QUESTIONS WITHIN.

- I WILL USE THE POWER OF THE MAGICAL RANDOM AVAFLICKTHRU TO SELECT THE MOST RELEVANT QUESTION FOR MY PRESENT STATE .

- I WILL TAKE A WALK THROUGH THE CORRIDORS OF MY MIND WITH A CROWBAR READY TO OPEN ANY AND ALL LOCKED DOORS.

If you can commit to these noble and courageous values then by all means you are welcome to join the society of truth and self knowledge. Copy out the following statement in your own handwriting:

I pledge my allegiance to the cult of B.A.W.

Now you may proceed. Keep the faith. And select a page at random.

(Or is it selecting you . . ?)

BURN AFTER WRITING
TEEN

BURN AFTER WRITING

THE TRUTH

Repeat after me - I promise to try really hard to tell mainly the truth, almost the whole truth and hardly anything but the truth so help me dog, fingers crossed across my heart and hope to die, times infinity, no returns.

You can't hide from the truth but it sure can hide from you. It's not easy to see yourself clearly. Let's face it - you are pretty biased. But it is fun to try and think about yourself as truthfully as possible. Even if sometimes you have to come at the task from a random angle to trick yourself into telling the truth.

Try not to lie to the book. The book will not judge you. Be brave. Nobody ever has to read this but you. (Unless you leave it somewhere dumb accidentally on purpose).

Burn After Writing. Or not...

Good luck.

HASTA LA VISTA
Baby

THE PAST

THE PAST

You are on the bridge between two worlds. Behind you is the merry land of childhood, ahead the shimmering city of adulthood. Below you is a river full of crocodiles. There are many distractions on the bridge. What do you want to do now?

You know you're growing up when you suddenly realise you're just not that excited about sweets anymore. (This doesn't happen for everyone, and excludes Haribo) Looking back it's easy to get all nostalgic for being a kid. But remember how much you always wanted to be older when you were a kid?

The best way to honour your childhood self is to make yourself into the most awesome being you could ever have imagined. Ask yourself - would my childhood self think that what I am doing now is staggeringly awesome? If the answer is yes, you are winning.

Answer the questions about your past, you'll never be able to remember your childhood as clearly as you can now, then you'll have a treasure trove of memories kept safe in this book forever.

THE PAST

Take a walk through the garden of memory into the hazy half
remembered days of your personal history.
Everybody's talking about the good old days...

My earliest memory

When I was younger, I dreamt of becoming

When I look into the past, the thing I miss the most

My childhood described in one word

My best friend growing up

The single most profound act of kindness that I will never forget

The first song I ever remember hearing

The teacher who has had the most influence on my life so far

The long lost childhood possession that I would like to see again

My favourite bedtime story as a child

A list of countries I have visited

Last TV programme I watched

The most expensive thing I've ever bought

If I could have lived through any time period, it would have been

The first thing I bought with my own money

The hardest thing I've ever done

The worst thing I've ever eaten

The piece of music I loved as a child

The craziest thing I have ever done in my life

The 4 best times I've ever had in my life

1 _____

2 _____

3 _____

4 _____

If I could spend 48 hours with anyone (living or dead), it would it be (and we would)

My favourite phone photo

3 things that I have always wanted to do but have never done.

1 _____

2 _____

3 _____

A time when I broke the rules

The 3 things have I accomplished in the last 12 months that I am most proud of

1 _____

2 _____

3 _____

If I could go back in time and witness any historical event, it would be

My biggest disappointment

The sweets I loved when I was younger

The stupidest thing I have ever done

My best EPIC WIN

My worst EPIC FAIL

The one thing I'll never forget

The most #YOLO thing I've done

The most #FML thing that has happened to me

MY FIRSTS #1

"When was the last time you did something for the first time?"

First friend

_____

First song bought

_____

First holiday

_____

First gig/concert

_____

First teacher

_____

First pet

_____

First thing I learnt to cook

_____

First place I lived

_____

First school

_____

THE LAST WORD

Fleeting moments fly past us whistling in the wind. Can you catch one out of the air like Mr Miyagi catching flies with chopsticks in the original Karate Kid (not the remake)?

Last movie

_____

Last book

_____

Last gig

_____

Last time I cried

_____

Last time I laughed

_____

Last song I listened to

_____

Last time I was scared

_____

Last time I danced

_____

THESE ARE A FEW OF MY FAVOURITE THINGS

When you like something so much you feel like you might go crazy.
When you wish there was a love button on Facebook. What you like
says a lot about you!

1 tv show I love that was made more than ten years ago

3 of the most recent films I have watched

4 people from history that I find interesting

My **5** favourite things to eat

My **3** favourite things to drink

 # MY TOP 5 (of all time)

MY TOP  BANDS

MY TOP 5 ALBUMS

MY TOP  SONGS

MY TOP 🟊 BOOKS

MY TOP  MOVIES

MY TOP  FAVOURITE PLACES IN THE WORLD

MY TOP  TV PROGRAMMES

MY TOP  CELEBRITIES

My Life in Trivia

Birthplace _____

Living now _____

Currently wearing _____

Siblings _____

Height _____

Star sign _____

Pet _____

Magazine _____

Drink _____

Breakfast _____

Starter _____

Main course _____

Dessert _____

Snack _____

Restaurant _____

Fast Food _____

Designer _____

Clothing _____

Shoes _____

Car _____

Phone _____

Camera _____

Dream job _____

Shop _____

Comfort food _____

Word _____

Hobby _____

Colour _____

Sport _____

Team _____

Game _____

Website _____

TV programme _____

THE PRESENT

THE PRESENT

Oh that crazy present moment, when everything happens and yet it always seems like it's slipping through your fingers, it's happening to someone else or it's happening somewhere else leaving you in some boring everyday reality that you can't control.

Except every now and then when it becomes totally brilliant and everything seems to make sense and be worthwhile. But you don't know how it happened or how to get it back.

Live for the now or plan for the future? Everybody seems to have their own idea. Everybody tells you these are the best days of your life. So much pressure! They're all wrong. Be where you are. Nobody else is really having any more fun than you are, they're all just pretending.

It's all precious, it's all trash; it doesn't matter - it all matters; it's just that trivial holy moment pulsating through infinity.

Where is your head at right now?

And now?

And now?

And now?

And now?

THE PRESENT

NOW! NOW! NOW! It's still now. Yep, it's still now. When is it? IT'S NOW!
Still now. Still now. Yep. Still now. We can keep going. You keep reading,
we'll keep doing it. Still now. Still now.

A selfie I took

RIGHT HERE RIGHT NOW

Feeling _____

Wearing _____

Wanting _____

Needing _____

Thinking _____

Loving _____

Hating _____

Craving _____

The cartoon character that I resemble the most

The song that makes me want to dance

My username

My favourite subject

My favourite Apps

My favourite blogs

My favourite colour

My style

My most prized possession

Today I learnt

Three things that I am really bad at

MY PARTY PLAYLIST

MY CHILL OUT MIX TAPE

Four things that I enjoy

Three things that bore me

Two things that confuse me

The one thing that people take way too seriously

My hero is

The person I owe an apology to

My least favourite musical genre

The biggest inspiration in my life

Things I collect

My hidden talent

If a genie granted me 3 wishes, they would be

1 _____

2 _____

3 _____

The first 5 songs that play when I press shuffle

1 _____

2 _____

3 _____

4 _____

5 _____

If I was a superhero my name would be

If I could have a conversation today with one person from history,
it would be with

The one relationship I need to fix

Two things that make me happy

If I could be anywhere in the world right now

My favourite little things to enjoy in life

If I could give one thing to one person it would be

My greatest fear

If I didn't know how old I was, I would think I was

The geekiest thing about me

A new skill I'd like to learn

If I could change my first name, I would change it to

If I could change one thing about my parents, it would be

My personal style summed up in 3 words

The one movie that I could watch over and over again

If I could drop any subject it would be

How old is old

If I could go to the fridge right now and find one thing

The one thing I don't mind spending proper money on

If I had a brainwashing machine, I would use it on

The song I love to sing along to

Two things that annoy me

If I could clean up one mess, it would be

If I could choose to stay a certain age forever, it would be

If I had £5000 to spend, I would you spend it on

If I had to be trapped in a TV show for a month, it would be

The first song to come into my head right now

If I could have any pet it would be

If I was to win the lottery, this amount would be enough

I need to forgive

If I could pick up the phone and call one person, living or dead, right now, it would be

Things I can't live without

My favourite way to spend a Saturday Night

Five things I never knew about my parents (until after I asked them)

1. _____

2. _____

3. _____

4. _____

5. _____

If I could make one thing vanish forever, it would be

The famous person that people tell me I resemble

My top 5 websites

1. _____

2. _____

3. _____

4. _____

5. _____

If my house was on fire, the three things I would grab

1. _____

2. _____

3. _____

If I was uber-rich, this is where I would go on holiday

My parents in 4 words

If I was given £10,000 today on the condition that I couldn't keep the money for myself, I would . . .

Right now, at this moment, the thing I want the most

If I had to take one person with me on a deserted island it would be

If I had to sing one Karaoke tune in crowded bar of strangers,
my song would be

The most valuable thing I own

The song title that best describes my life.

My friends for life

Things that I am currently craving

Something I do that makes me feel proud of myself

One gadget that the world is missing

3 things that cheer me up

If I could only eat one meal for the rest of my life it would be

If I had to have a tattoo, it would be

The funniest person I know

The person who has the hardest life I know

The place I would love to live

My five favourite words in the English language

The four lamest words in the English language

My three favourite foreign words

The % of time I spend thinking about things I want to get

The % of time I spend thinking about things I already have

Three things that make me angry

Things that I feel are injustices in the world

If I could make one thing disappear it would be

If I could take my friends on amazing holiday this is what we would do

The title of my autobiography

The song that sums up the story of my life so far

The song that always makes me cry

The three best things about being me (and one worst)

My favourite day of the week

My biggest distractions

The single biggest source of drama in my life

My latest obsession

The thing that I long for the most

The things that I do that are unique and original

The place I would rather be right now

If I could trade lives with one person

The advert which is currently annoying me the most

The worst 3 songs I've ever heard

My favourite album cover

The one person who just doesn't get me

The one thing that everybody seems to love that I just don't get

The worst movie I've ever seen

A pie chart showing my activities in an average week
(eg. homework, school, internet)

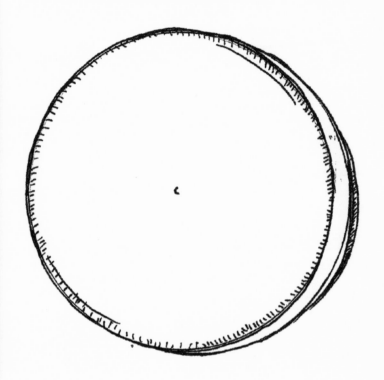

Things that make me laugh

If I could direct the Hollywood movie of my life story,
this would be the cast list

_____ as _____me_____

_____ as _____

_____ as _____

_____ as _____

_____ as _____

_____ as _____

_____ as _____

The title of the movie of my life

The song for the main theme of the movie of my life

The song for the opening credits of the movie of my life

The song for the closing titles of the movie of my life

Three things that I'm rubbish at

My favourite way to spend a weekend

The most exciting four things in the world

The most boring three things in the world

Success (in 3 words)

1. _____

2. _____

3. _____

If I woke up and found myself invisible I would

The person I feel most comfortable talking about anything to

The world's biggest diva

My BFF

RATE MY TEACHER

Subject	Marks out of 10
English	
Maths	
History	
Science	
Geography	
Art	
PE	
Music	
Languages	
Technology	

The time I would wake up if it was up to me

6 am ◯   7 am ◯

8 am ◯   9 am ◯

12 noon ◯   1 pm ◯

A haiku (by me)

My favourite Youtube clip

My favourite Youtuber

If I opened my own nightclub it would be called

The one song that I'm sick of hearing

The one thing I want that I think is way too expensive

The city I would like to live in

The maximum amount of time I could go without using my phone

The maximum amount of time I could go without using the internet

The maximum amount of time I could go without texting someone

The shops that I always have go into when I'm out

Things that confuse me

The book I'm currently reading

The album I'm currently listening to

My weird habits

Three things that I'm over

5 things I need in my life

1 _____

2 _____

3 _____

4 _____

5 _____

5 things I want in my life

1 _____

2 _____

3 _____

4 _____

5 _____

My Creativity Board

A collage (by me)

My Friend Map

Put yourself in the middle of a spider diagram and map out all your friendships. Put stronger lines for stronger bonds.

MY ALL TIME FAVOURITES

Song

_____

Album

_____

Gig

_____

Place

_____

Movie

_____

Book

_____

Band

_____

Holiday

_____

City

_____

Teacher

_____

Word

_____

TV Programme

_____

Actor/Actress

_____

Food

_____

School Subject

_____

Colour

_____

Number

_____

Sport

_____

Scary Movie

_____

Animal

_____

I love...

I love...

LET'S BE HONEST

(The first word that comes into your head)

I am

_____

I am not

_____

I adore

_____

I detest

_____

I have

_____

I have never

_____

I like

_____

I don't like

_____

I love

_____

I hate

_____

I need _____

I want _____

I can _____

I can't _____

I'm always _____

I'm never _____

I'm afraid of _____

I'm not afraid to _____

I'm pretty good at _____

I'm rubbish at _____

I want more _____

I want less _____

Life on the line

Circle one of the two characteristics on each line that you feel best describes your personality.

Apprehensive	Calm
Single Minded	Flexible
Fearless	Cautious
Pensive	Carefree
See big picture	Detail obsessed
Competitive	Laid back
Fast	Slow
Relaxed	Impatient
Introvert	Extrovert

If I had to wear a t-shirt with one word on it for the rest of my life

I am sick to death of hearing about

My secret skill

The one thing that I do that I would like to be able to stop

Lyrics that
I love...

(and that mean something to me)

My favourite thinkers, doers, believers, legends, dreamers
(and people who basically rock)

POSERS

Losers, fools, airheads, fakes, randomers!
(and people I would like to punch in the face)

PEOPLE
who mean something to me

PLACES
that mean something to me

PRICELESS

The things that money just can't buy... £ £
£ £
£

JUDGEMENT DAY

Be honest. You judge everybody you meet. We all do.
How about judging yourself for a change?

Honesty   /10

Intelligence   /10

Generosity   /10

Talent   /10

Forgiveness   /10

Confidence   /10

Happiness   /10

Humbleness   /10

Loyalty   /10

Loving   /10

Uniqueness   /10

Fashionable   /10

Humour   /10

DEFACE TO FACE

Cut out photographs from a magazine and deface them
with a black biro. Paste the best ones here.

THIS iS HoW It fEeLs

Get a newspaper or magazine
and remix the headlines
with scissors and glue
that shows how you feel today!

WORD ASSOCIATION

When I say life, you say what ❓

Don't think; just write the first word that comes into your head. Let your subconscious mind do the talking. You might be surprised at what you discover about yourself through the magical power of randomicity.

Life	_____
School	_____
Fame	_____
Sadness	_____
Love	_____
Family	_____
Age	_____
Friends	_____
Parents	_____
Success	_____
Fear	_____
Home	_____
Future	_____
Failure	_____
Destiny	_____
Humour	_____
Envy	_____
Honesty	_____

FAMILY IS

NEVER STOP
dreaming

THE FUTURE

THE FUTURE

If there was a book with your whole future written in it in the library - would you read it?

Is that even possible?

The following questions are about your future. Given that you have absolutely no idea what will happen in your future you are advised to simply make the answers up. And if you can't do that then just imagine that you can.

In life you write your own future, but then people come along and edit it for you so you never get quite what you asked for. Making decisions about your future is like writing a Christmas list in a language that Santa doesn't understand and can't be bothered to learn because he's busy with a billion other lists.

You should answer these questions anyway, because there is nothing funnier than reading predictions you made about your life ten years ago.

May your happiness take you by surprise!

THE FUTURE

Let's play the predictions game! What do you want from the future?

The 3 things have I been putting off that I need to do before the end of the year

1. _____

2. _____

3. _____

My next challenge

The one thing that I am not looking forward to

My goals

My perfect gap year

The one thing I could be famous for

When I leave school I would like to

10 things I would like to try

1

2

3

4

5

6

7

8

9

10

BOOKS I WANT TO READ

THESE SONGS ARE THE SOUNDTRACK TO MY LIFE

The one thing I'm most excited about

The next big thing in fashion should be

I LOVE YOU ♡

Learn to say I love you in three languages. Write them here.

THE FUTURE STARTS HERE...

In one week from now I will

In one month from now I will

In one year from now I will

In 10 years from now I will

In 25 years from now I will

In 50 years from now I will

A LETTER TO MY FUTURE SELF

Do not read until .... (10 years from now)

DEAR SELF

YOURS TRULY

The Bucket List

You want to live forever!
But you have to admit it's unlikely.
So what are the things you absolutely have to do?

Tick them off this list and then start your own:

1. Ski/snowboard
2. Canoe
3. Ride a camel
4. Play a musical instrument
5. Learn to dance
6. Visit London
7. Ride in a hot air balloon
8. Scuba dive
9. Ride a unicorn
10. Go white water rafting
11. Make pottery
12. Paint a picture
13. Write a short story
14. Write a book
15. Go camping
16. Climb a mountain
17. Plant a tree
18. Fly in a helicopter

19. Go hiking
20. Visit Paris
21. Give to charity
22. Go rock climbing
23. Learn to juggle
24. Find my thing
25. Learn to knit
26. Go bowling
27. Make a music video
28. Break a world record
29. Learn origami
30. Fly to the moon
31. See an eclipse
32. Visit New York
33. Watch the sun set
34. Plan a gap year
35. Ride a horse

My Bucket List

1.

2.

3.

4.

5.

6.

7.

8.

9.

10

I WISH . . .

Are you the kind of person that wishes for things that kind of make sense or crazy things that probably wouldn't even work? Or are you the kind of person that wishes for limitless wishes?

(That kind of ruins the game.)

You can have one or the other but not both.
It's crunch time. Make a decision!

The ride or The destination
Mac or PC
Rich or Famous
Sweet or Salted
Snapchat or Instagram
Dance or Hip Hop
Pepsi or Coke
London or New York
Amusement Park or Water Park
Nike or Adidas
Movies or Music
Late Night or Early Morning
Dog or Cat
Summer or Winter
City or Country
See the future or Change the past
Las Vegas or Paris
Facebook or Twitter
Going out or Staying in
iPhone or Samsung

Subway or McDonalds

Watch the movie or Read the book

Spirituality or Religion

Pinterest or Tumblr

Mountains or Beach

Odd or Even

Appetizer or Dessert

Adventure or Relaxation

Phone or Text

Celebrity or Artist

Slow or Fast

Head or Heart

Soup or Salad

Brains or Beauty

Fame or Money

Talent or Skill

Creativity or Knowledge

Art or Science

Freedom or Security

Vampires or Werewolves

Funny or Powerful

Pencil or Pen

Cupcake or Cookie

Bath or Shower

Chocolate or Chips

Past or Future

Sunrise or Sunset

DJ or Band

New or Old

MOST LIKELY TO...

From my friends the one most likely to be a:

Politician _____

Fashion Guru _____

Rock Star _____

Doctor _____

Bestselling Novelist _____

Olympic Medalist _____

Millionaire _____

Famous Artist _____

Oscar Winner _____

WAG _____

Nobel Prize Winner _____

Top Model _____

Teacher _____

World Record Breaker _____

Scientist _____

Vet _____

Serial Killer _____

Pro Wrestler _____

Be on TV _____

Marry a Millionaire _____

MY ALTERNATIVE YEARBOOK

And the winner is:

Class Clown _____

Teachers Pet _____

Funniest Laugh _____

Loudest _____

Quietest _____

Happiest _____

Most Creative _____

Most Annoying _____

Most Competitive _____

Best Dressed _____

Best Musician _____

Best Double Act _____

Bossiest _____

Best Singer _____

Most Friendly _____

Biggest Drama Queen _____

Biggest Party Animal _____

Blondest _____

Biggest Geek _____

THE ORACLE

Draw around your hand, fill it with predictions for your future.

QUICK

Googled my own name ( ) Won a trophy ( ) Learnt a foreign language ( ) Been to a spa ( ) Ridden in a limo ( ) Flown in a plane ( ) Met someone famous ( ) Memorised a poem ( ) Broken something expensive ( ) Sponsored a child ( ) Danced with my mother/father ( ) Jumped off the high board ( ) Dived off the high board ( ) Had an invisible friend ( ) Sung karaoke ( ) Been on TV ( ) Given money to a street beggar ( ) Written something in wet cement ( ) Sent a message in a bottle ( ) Know at least one good joke ( ) Written poetry ( ) Performed on stage ( ) Caught a fish ( ) Grown a plant ( ) Volunteered for charity ( ) Been ice skating ( ) Been zorbing ( ) Learnt a card trick ( ) Had a penpal ( ) Eaten sushi ( ) Done the splits ( ) Broken a bone ( ) Been trick or treating ( ) Seen a fox ( ) Eaten with chopsticks ( )

FIRE

Got an A in any subject ( ) Fired a bow and arrow ( ) Ridden a roller coaster ( ) Given clothes to charity ( ) Been to a funeral ( ) Ridden a mechanical bull ( ) Owned a pet ( ) Dyed my hair ( ) Made a stop frame animation movie ( ) Been to a fancy dress party ( ) Got an F in any subject ( ) Cooked dinner for my parents ( ) Cheated in a test ( ) Released a paper lantern ( ) Ignored a friend request ( ) Chased a rainbow ( ) Followed a trail ( ) Learnt to read music ( ) Had a job ( ) Started my own blog ( ) Skipped school ( ) Feigned an illness ( ) Sung in a choir ( ) Pimped my phone ( ) Learnt a martial art ( ) Seen a shooting star ( ) Been skiing ( ) Baked a cake ( ) Ridden a horse ( ) Slept under the stars ( ) Solved Rubiks Cube ( ) Been part of a flash mob ( ) Made a Mentos rocket ( )

I want...

LESS

I want...
MORE ✚

You have thirteen minutes to write the lyrics for a song called

IT'S MY LIFE

Set the timer. Go!

VOW NOW

Circle your pledges, and add your own

Take chances

TRY HARDER WITH MY PARENTS

SAY NO   TELL THE TRUTH

        BE RANDOM

                    SAY I LOVE YOU

        Say thanks

                            LAUGH OUT LOUD

Apologize

        LAUGH MORE

                                    LIVE MORE

                    REGRET LESS

HAVE MORE FUN

        Speak my mind

                                    WORRY LESS

                    SMILE MORE

Accept criticism

            TAKE RESPONSIBILITY

LISTEN MORE

        DON'T HATE

                                    READ MORE

            Work harder

EMBRACE CHANGE

                            Feel good anyway

Worry less

Start a journal

WRITE EVERYDAY

TAKE MORE DUMB PICTURES

Accept criticism

Take responsibility

LISTEN & LOVE

SMILE MORE

Embrace change

HAVE NO REGRETS

SLEEP MORE

MAKE ART

Eat good food

GIVE CREDIT, TAKE BLAME

FORGIVE MYSELF FOR MY MISTAKES

LIGHTEN UP

Relax more

PRIORITISE

TAKE CHANCES

SAY NO

APOLOGISE

Travel more

DREAM BIG

SHAKE THINGS UP

BE THANKFUL

TREAT MYSELF

HELP OTHERS

BE ME

MY MOOD BOARD

Collage My Life

Would I rather?

Eat a plate of wichety grubs or a dish of fish eyeballs

Spend the night in a graveyard or in an abandoned house

Go back in time or forward in time

Be 3ft 6in tall or 7ft 6in tall

Be happy but poor or be rich and miserable

Fart classical music or belch heavy metal

Have a pet crocodile or a pet tiger

Speak only in rhyme or sing every word

Dress exclusively in 70s clothing or only in 60s clothing

Be phoneless or computer less

Only eat cereal or toast

Sleep on a bed of nails or walk on hot coals

Have bad breath or greasy hair

Have billy bob teeth or a mullet

Talk extra loud or extra quiet

Have x-ray vision or bionic hearing

Never eat fast food again or eat fast food all the time

Snore in my sleep or talk in my sleep

Be half my height or double my weight

Talk like Dobbie or like Gollum

Give up the internet forever or TV forever

One wish today or 3 wishes in 10 years time

Be a movie star or a Nobel Prize winning scientist

Smell like boiled cabbage or have tangerine orange skin

Have an extra long neck or extra long feet

Win £10,000 or have a 50% chance of winning £100,000

Be able to talk to animals or be fluent in every language

Be the most popular in school or the smartest in school

Stuck in the 70s or in the 80s

Sweat green slime or sneeze purple goo

Be able to read minds or see everyones future

Never brush my teeth again or never brush my hair again

Always laugh at sad things or always cry at funny things

Do a bungee jump or sing in front of 500 people

Do the dishes or tidy my room

Be a Youtube superstar or blog hero

Hear bad news first or bad news last

Morning person or night owl

Have a photographic memory or forget anything I wanted

Have a humungous nose or enormous elephant sized ears

Never eat chocolate again or never eat ice cream again

Age only from the neck up or only from the neck down

Spend every minute of the rest of my life indoors or outdoors

Be hairy all over or completely bald

See the future or change the past

MY FUTURE

Never at any time in your life will you get more sick to death of people talking about your future than now. Nobody knows what they want from their future. Some people pretend they do.
They're kidding themselves.

So relax.

To prove this point beyond all doubt try this experiment.
Write down a description of both your ideal job and perfect partner opposite. Keep this book somewhere safe.

When you finally nail your career and meet 'the one' refer back to your dream descriptions opposite and witness how completely and utterly wrong you were about absolutely everything.

We don't know what we really want.
We only think we do.

In this spirit of joyful ignorance, we can properly enjoy making wild predictions about the future free of any attempt to make them accurate.

My ideal career

My future partner

I KNOW EXACTLY WHO I AM, WHAT I WANT AND WHO I WANT TO BE!

(I think!)

BURN AFTER WRITING - THE TIME CAPSULE

Repeat after me . . .

I will not... mindlessly follow orders

Now forget that and do as I tell you. Because I am you.
I am the voice in your head.

You will come back to this book when thirteen years have passed
and do all the exercises again.

Then you can meet yourself, like in that weird dream you keep having
(only considerably more interesting).

Congratulations truth seeker!
You reached the end of the vision quest.

AFK TILL I DIE

*AFK – away from the keyboard